BLAST OFF!

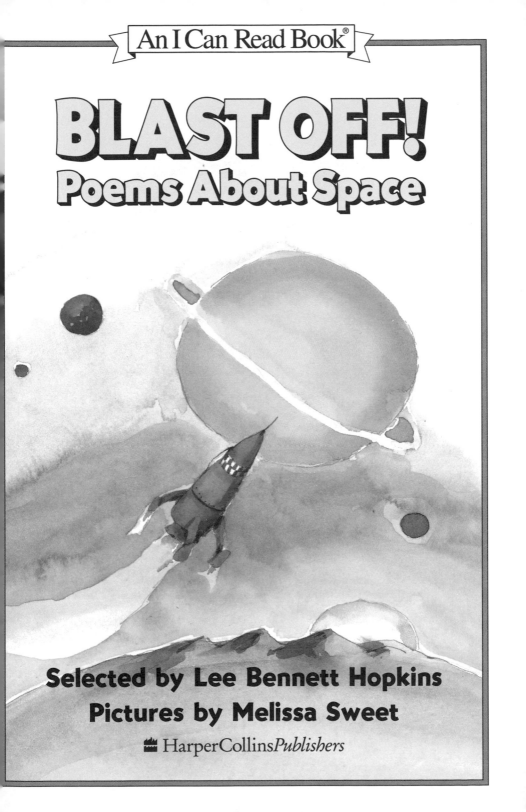

BLAST OFF!
Poems About Space

Selected by Lee Bennett Hopkins
Pictures by Melissa Sweet

HarperCollins*Publishers*

Blast Off!
Poems About Space
Text copyright © 1995 by Lee Bennett Hopkins
Illustrations copyright © 1995 by Melissa Sweet
Printed in the U.S.A. All rights reserved.

Library of Congress Cataloging-in-Publication Data
Blast off! : poems about space / selected by Lee Bennett Hopkins ; pictures by
Melissa Sweet.
p.   cm.
Summary: A collection of poems about the moon, stars, planets, astronauts,
and related wonders.
ISBN 0-06-024260-4. — ISBN 0-06-024261-2 (lib. bdg.)
1. Outer space—Juvenile poetry. 2. Children's poetry, American. [1. Outer
space—Poetry. 2. American poetry—Collections.] I. Hopkins, Lee Bennett.
II. Sweet, Melissa, ill. III. Title. IV. Series.
PS595.O87B53   1995   93-24536
811'.5408036—dc20   CIP
                                                                AC

Typography by Christine Hoffman
5   6   7   8   9   10
❖

ACKNOWLEDGMENTS

Every effort has been made to trace ownership of all copyrighted material and to secure the necessary permissions to reprint these selections. In the event of any question arising as to the use of any material, the editor and the publisher, while expressing regret for any inadvertent error, will make the necessary correction in future printings.

Thanks are due to the following for permission to reprint the works listed below:

Curtis Brown, Ltd., for "Blast Off!" by Lee Bennett Hopkins. Copyright © 1995 by Lee Bennett Hopkins; "Last Laugh" by Lee Bennett Hopkins. Copyright © 1974 by Lee Bennett Hopkins; "Letter to the Moon" by Jane Yolen. Copyright © 1993 by Jane Yolen. All reprinted by permission of Curtis Brown, Ltd.

Brod Bagert for "Children of the Sun." Used by permission of the author, who controls all rights.

Barbara Juster Esbensen for "The Milky Way." Used by permission of the author, who controls all rights.

Lillian M. Fisher for "The Moon." Used by permission of the author, who controls all rights.

HarperCollins Publishers, for "Song" from Sing to the Sun by Ashley Bryan. Copyright © 1992 by Ashley Bryan; "Shooting Stars" from Always Wondering by Aileen Fisher. Copyright © 1991 by Aileen Fisher; excerpt from "Counting" from Dogs & Dragons, Trees & Dreams by Karla Kuskin. Copyright © 1980 by Karla Kuskin. All reprinted by permission of HarperCollins Publishers.

Bobbi Katz for "When I'm an Astronaut." Copyright © 1995 by Bobbi Katz. Used with permission of the author.

J. Patrick Lewis for "A Black Hole" and "First Moon Landing." Used by permission of the author, who controls all rights.

Macmillan Publishing Company, for "The Falling Star" from Collected Poems of Sara Teasdale. Copyright 1930 by Sara Teasdale Filsinger, renewed 1958 by Guaranty Trust Company of New York. Reprinted with permission of Macmillan Publishing Company.

Joanne Oppenheim for an excerpt from Have You Seen Roads? (Young Scott Books). Copyright © 1969 by Joanne Oppenheim.

Leslie D. Perkins for "Moonlight." Used by permission of the author, who controls all rights.

Marian Reiner for "A Meteorite" and "Outer Space Wondering" by Sandra Liatsos. Copyright © 1995 by Sandra Liatsos. "Space Song" from There Is No Rhyme for Silver by Eve Merriam. Copyright © 1962 by Eve Merriam. Copyright renewed 1990 by Eve Merriam. All reprinted by permission of Marian Reiner.

Sarah Wilson for "Lullaby." Used by permission of the author, who controls all rights.

To Faye Johnston
and
Kaye Johnston—

Teachers who reach
toward the stars.
LBH

To Marcella and Steve
MS

BLAST OFF!

by Lee Bennett Hopkins

A rocket ship

will take you far

to see a crater,

quasar,

star,

constellations—

brilliant, bright—

8

a planet,

comet,

meteorite—

Blast off, child,

it's

time

for

flight.

WHEN I'M AN ASTRONAUT

by Bobbi Katz

First I'll get into my spacesuit.

Then I'll bravely wave good-by.

Next I'll climb into my spacecraft

Built to sail right through the sky!

In command inside the capsule,

I will talk to ground control.

When we've checked out

　　all the systems,

I'll say, "Let the countdown roll!"

And it's 4-3-2-1—blast off—

With a smile upon my face,

I'll spin loops around the planets

up, up, up in outer space!

LAST LAUGH

by Lee Bennett Hopkins

They all laughed when I told them
I wanted to be

A woman in space
Floating so free.

But they won't laugh at me
When they finally see
My feet up on Mars
And my face on TV.

FIRST MOON LANDING

by J. Patrick Lewis

Two highfliers,

Buzz and Neil,

Said they couldn't

Wait to feel

Just what kind of

Moon it was—

"Take a look around,"

Said Buzz.

Open the hatch

And out the door,

Down the ladder

To the moonlit floor.

After he had

Sunk his heel

Into the dusty

Ocean, Neil

Knew what a lovely

Moon it was—

"One small step . . ."

Said Neil to Buzz.

LETTER TO THE MOON

by Jane Yolen

Dear Old Moon:

Your new moon face

Has human footprints every place.

The astronauts did not take care

And walked upon you everywhere.

But worse, they left behind a mess

That surely causes you distress.

Forgive us, moon,

Please keep your glow.

With love,

From all of us

below.

THE MOON

by *Lillian M. Fisher*

The moon has no light

of its own.

It's cold and dark

and dead as stone,

But it catches light

from the burning sun

And shows itself

When each day is done.

MOONLIGHT

by Leslie D. Perkins

On

the

dark

lawn

is a

pale

moon

path

just

for

me

SONG

by Ashley Bryan

Sing to the sun

It will listen

And warm your words

Your joy will rise

Like the sun

And glow

Within you

Sing to the moon

It will hear

And soothe your cares

Your fears will set

Like the moon

And fade

Within you

CHILDREN OF THE SUN

by Brod Bagert

Mercury's small

Almost nothing at all.

Venus is bright and near.

Earth is a place with deep blue seas

And a sky that is blue and clear.

Mars is red and angry.

Jupiter has an eye.

Saturn has rings of ice and stone
That circle round its sky.

Uranus, Neptune, and Pluto
Are far away and cold.

So now I know my planets
And I'm only six years old.

SPACE SONG

by *Eve Merriam*

Jupiter, Saturn, Uranus, Mars;

Here we go whizzing around the stars.

Venus, Neptune, Mercury,

And oh, Pluto—

What on Earth do you see?

How little Earth looks down below:

What tiny creatures they must grow.

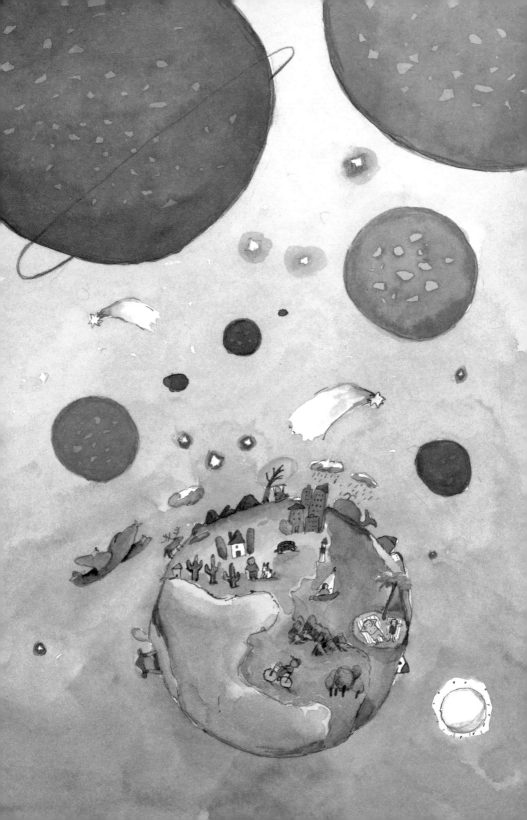

THE FALLING STAR

by Sara Teasdale

I saw a star slide down the sky,

Blinding the north as it went by,

Too burning and too quick to hold,

Too lovely to be bought or sold,

Good only to make wishes on

And then forever to be gone.

SHOOTING STARS

by Aileen Fisher

When stars get loosened

in their sockets,

they shoot off through

the night like rockets.

But though I stay

and watch their trip

and search where they

have seemed to slip,

I never yet have found a CHIP

to carry in my pockets.

A METEORITE

by Sandra Liatsos

A fireball

came roaring down

from far in outer space.

That fireball exploded!

Its pieces ran a race,

till one crashed down

in my backyard

and made a great big hole,

that looks as if

a giant lost

his mother's mixing bowl!

A BLACK HOLE

by J. Patrick Lewis

A star that's just

　　Too fat to hang

Far out in space

　　May pop—and bang!

Its insides get

　　So blazing hot—

One day it's there,

　　The next it's not!

And no one knows

Exactly why

But in the ceiling

Of the sky,

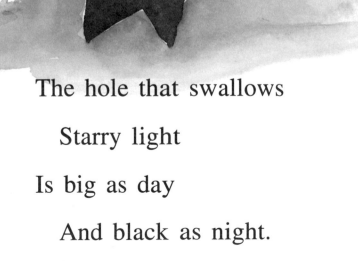

The hole that swallows

Starry light

Is big as day

And black as night.

THE MILKY WAY

by Barbara Juster Esbensen

Who spilled

these stars

across the sky

like

sparkling dust

like

clouds of light?

They pour their

milky shine

into the deep black

bowl

above our heads

white

glittering

too many to

count.

from **COUNTING**

by Karla Kuskin

Counting the stars

As they glitter bright white

Is lovely indeed

And a marvelous sight

When the air is as fresh

As the first night in fall.

But I always have a feeling

That comes very softly stealing

When my head with stars is reeling

That I didn't count them all.

STAR

by Anonymous

Star light,

Star bright,

First star I see tonight,

I wish I may,

I wish I might

Have the wish

I wish tonight.

OUTER SPACE WONDERING

by Sandra Liatsos

Who knows how many

miles there are

far in outer space?

Who knows what wondrous

creatures

we might meet face-to-face.

Who knows what giant worlds

are spinning round a star?

Who knows if a distant people

wonder where we are?

LULLABY

by Sarah Wilson

Goodnight,

goodnight

to friends in space

and those on ships

that interlace

with suns and moons

across the sea

of light

that rims

our galaxy.

Goodnight,

goodnight

to all who fly

and those who seek

new worlds in sky

from my home planet

swirled in blue

a long and peaceful

calm to you.

BLAST OFF!

by Joanne Oppenheim

Wheelless

wingless

weightless

unknown roads in space await us.

Index of Authors and Titles